Brief & Bleeding Margins

Praise for *Brief & Bleeding Margins*

Throughout *Brief & Bleeding Margins* Marissa Forbes gifts her readers with a raw and unapologetic coming-to-self tale of a cis-queer-woman whose hyphens were muted by oppression for far too long. This collection is a Matryoshka doll, with each chapter challenging layers and layers of societal expectations thrust upon her over a lifetime. Poem by poem, the reader follows Forbes as she exposes these gender roles and the writer's true essence (new-found, re-discovered, re-claimed) to finally take up space in both life and in honest writing. Once you reach the final doll, there's the poet. And her poetry. You'll feel the love for her children and her hatred of the patriarchy. *Brief & Bleeding Margins* is the coming-to-self journey every contemporary woman wonders if she is going through alone. Forbes puts the mirror up, holds your hand, and shows you that you're not alone.

— Larissa Freitas (she/her), author of *Shaped* and *Viva, by Definition*

Marissa Forbes' *Brief & Bleeding Margins* is a fearless collection of poems and lyric essays with titles that take the current trend of long titles and turns it up to 12. She muses on American politics and its attempt to slap laws on the body of anyone who isn't a cis white man. She asks readers to question what it means to be "sexy" and highlights the way identity (perceived and actual) origamis itself into it all. Forbes calls us to bear witness to everything that being a mother and creative person means in this world. In these pages, there is grit and grief, self-forgiveness and self-love, in spite of a country and government determined to shove us all into broken boxes. Forbes's voice is relatable, unafraid, and puts rhythm to what we're all thinking. These poems and the clever way Forbes turns a phrase will have you chewing on your own preconceived perceptions long after reading. And most importantly, you will know you're not alone.

— Sarah Herrin (they/them), Editor-in-Chief of Beyond the Veil Press, author of *The Oceanography of Her* and *Anti-Muse*

In *Brief & Bleeding Margins* Marissa Forbes has an innate ability to create a mindset of affirmations by not keeping silent about her feelings, which rise up from emotions so strongly embedded in her own truth and the truth of many as she becomes their voice, their despair told, their secrets unsilenced by what she sets forth to unbury. She creates a sense of unison and consensus about what many experience but are unable to state as she deftly weaves poems from her concoction of syllables and stories. When we keep silent about wrong-doings and an unequal sense of balance we protect many more voices that keep us down, and Forbes is able to unleash power in her poems that become the contrast to that which is birthed in the future to oppress. The sense that she is that positive, unassailable, and robust force, who is filled with love for humanity is felt strongly in this amazing piece of work. Her collection draws you in and unfolds her wisdom with every single, transforming page.

— Estela Victoria-Cordero (she/her), author of *Huitzilopochtli*

Brief & Bleeding Margins

Poems & Lyric Essays by
Marissa Forbes

World Stage Press
Verse from the Village

World Stage Press
Verse from the Village

Brief & Bleeding Margins
©2023 Marissa Forbes
ISBN: 978-1-952952-58-6

First Edition, 2023

All rights reserved. No part of this publication may be reproduced, distributed, or transmitted in any form or by any means, including photocopying, recording, or other electronic or mechanical methods, without the prior written permission of the publisher, except in the case of brief quotations embodied in critical reviews and certain other noncommercial uses permitted by copyright law.

Printed in the United States of America

Edited by Matthew Feinstein & Ruddy Lopez
Cover Design by Shiva Nosrati
Layout Design by Monica Alverca & Emily Anne Evans

For anyone who reads these poems and says, "Yup" at least once.

For the malleable yet formidable.

Table of Contents

xiii   Preface

xv   A Note About the Titles

BLOODY POLITICS

4   **When You Didn't Tell Anyone...**
Just tell yourself

8   **When #PinkTax Trended...**
Pink, like my insides

10   **When Politicians Use Glory Holes...**
I whisper into tampons & toilet paper rolls

14   **When 3,000 Feet In The Sky Becomes...**
3,000 feet in the sky

16   **When Your Lifelong Best Friend Is Struggling To Get Pregnant...**
The GOP Rep from Texas said

18   **When You Learn The Roe V. Wade Baby...**
One woman, her womb:

20   **When The Earth Sprouted Cotton...**
Cotton. Before it was toxic

22   **When You Live In A "Click & Collect" World...**
Amazon has the Also Bought

24   **When The New York Times Keeps On...**
For the 99%, debt is a lemon meringue pie

EMERGING, BRIEFLY

28   **When This Poem Was Supposed To Be About A Real Flower...**
Only the world took me

30   **When Spring In Colorado Arrives...**
When I was younger, I ate plums

32   **When Sears Is For Deals & Grooming…**
     Remember his first little fib?

34   **When You Yell At Your Kids…**
     This can't be growing up

36   **When You Lived In Brooklyn For A Decade…**
     A beautiful woman and an ugly man

38   **When My College Roommate Fell In Love With A Gay Guy…**
     All starry-eyed, she giggles

40   **When A Blow-Up Doll…**
     My dad just died, so

44   **When You Begin Dating Again…**
     I prefer long hair

46   **When You've Seen The Tree…**
     There's never been a more beautiful mango

48   **When You Read An Article…**
     I was on birth control for nearly a decade

MOTHER'S BLOOD

52   **When Your R.E.M Cycle Is Interrupted…**
     I lie awhile then we're the same height

54   **When You Were Married To A Man Who Is Only Good At Cooking…**
     Look at sexy me

56   **When Your Ex-Mother-In-Law Buys You A 23andMe…**
     We talk about being on the wrong side of history

58   **When You're Beyond House Poor…**
     Slabs of stones, uneven & broken

60   **When Death Is A Mushroom…**
     From root & stem to full blown slim-covered cap

62   **When Your Children's Father Left…**
     I let the lawn burn to a crip corn yellow

64   **When You Post A Facebook Status About Eating…**
     I can eat again: for my mind, body, & heart

66   **When Motherhood Is A Pie…**
     Melt ½ cup butter then fold in chopped windows of time

68	**When Learning To /rip/...**
	I must not have known
72	**When Your Second Child Wasn't Hard On Your Body...**
	First my belly
76	**When Your Oldest Child Declares *He* Will Be A *They*...**
	I was asked
78	**When Cavities Are A Right Of Passage...**
	You made your way through my mouth
80	**When You Give Yourself A Stick 'N' Poke...**
	On my forearm, tiny dots are poked one at a time
82	**When You Write A Poem For Dave Grohl...**
	When I was younger, I had a weakness for musicians
84	**When Your Husband Has An Affair...**
	Mornings are my addiction

BRIEF META-POESY

88	**When You Curse Your Muse...**
	Interruptions become wealthy without my muse
90	**When Insomnia Sits On Your Eyelids...**
	Your face gleams blue at night
92	**When You Read And Write Every Day...**
	On being a road
96	**When You Write A Poem Called "Just Enough"...**
	In the simple search for relief
98	**When You Leave Fingerprint Ink Stains...**
	A poet's fingerprints
100	**When *Praise For Poets* Becomes An Obligation...**
	Praise for poets: the ones with love like crimson
102	**When You're An Atheist...**
	People roll their chins toward hell when praying

105　Acknowledgements

Preface

Within a year and a half, I wrote two very personal poetry manuscripts, both wrapped tightly in a veil because I wasn't ready to fully expose my journey of heartbreak and healing through the lens of "all me, all 'I' all the time." I looked to history with *Bridging The Gap: Poems & Ethos For Emily Roebling* to tell my story of motherhood versus professional livelihood, intersectionality of sexism & racism, and the ramifications of a stifling marriage on one's dreams (published by Finishing Line Press). Then J.M Barrie's *Peter Pan* inspired my chapbook, *Surviving Peter Pan* (published by Beyond The Veil Press) where I personify all the survivors of Neverland to explore my own journey gaining freedom from an abusive narcissistic relationship.

Brief & Bleeding Margins represents the me that was literally written in the margins of those collections. These are the poems that slipped themselves into my notebooks through it all, and where I found my most authentic self. My true self unfolded as the themes emerged, and I saw myself in that space between the word and the red circle around it. I realized it is all *brief*, we all *bleed* (but women have more practice). I realized I was happy to finally see and fall in love with the "me" that lives in the margins of creation again.

Brief & Bleeding Margins is the rawest glimpse into my personal journey. "Brief" in the sense that readers glimpse smatterings of me through my short autobiographical prose that act as titles to the poems that follow. The poems dive headfirst into my opinions on my state of mind: on politics (BLOODY POLITICS), my emergence between girlhood-womanhood (EMERGING, BRIEFLY), my complicated but honest take on the pain and beauty of motherhood (MOTHER'S BLOOD), and finally the experience healing through the creative process (BRIEF META-POESY). "Bloody" in the sense that I allowed myself to be literal—as a woman: I bleed, and my existence holds that truth to be self-evident. Yet, I've never allowed myself to rip into the nitty-gritty of all that blood, of what layers womanhood really holds, until now. It also speaks to the truth that we all bleed, scab, heal, then bleed again…and again.

This collection should hit you in the gut as it opens the underbelly of American policy against women and its war on identity, whether it's of self, sexuality, family, or society (BLOODY POLITICS). It should scoop out your insides with its revelations on love and loss and all those often-disturbing experiences girls carry with them into womanhood (EMERGING, BRIEFLY). Your womb (or balls) should tighten as this collection moves into unabashed confessions of what motherhood is; because in all its beauty, it still leaves you bleeding with cuts of guilt or ambitions of perfection (MOTHER'S BLOOD). And finally, I want you hit with healing by means of creating your own grace and forgiveness because through all the pain and oozing, you still need optimism (BRIEF META-POESY). And for me, hope was opened again by reclaiming myself through these pieces.

Brief & Bleeding Margins is the most *me* any collection of poetry can be and even though it was written during a dark 18 months, it also created a space for growth, hope, and radical acceptance. This collection is meant to find the hurt and healing of the world, because truly we are, after all, just the marks in the margins—the scratches and swirls we make when trying to make our pen work again. We are works in progress and you will see yourself in my brief and bleeding history of now.

A Note on the Titles

Brief & Bleeding Margins took the trend of long titles and pushed it beyond ten. This isn't an experiment in lengthy titles just for the sake of length: They serve as self-revelations and conversations with the poems that follow. They're the rawest glimpse into my state of mind and I ask readers to enter the other side of a poet's consciousness when creating work. These titles hold a heavy space on the page because I aim to expose inspiration in all its brief & bleeding sparks. I hope to create an unabashed truth that blurs the line between vulnerability in healing and the uncomfortability of over-sharing. It is my intention that you, the reader, are overwhelmed by the smatterings of the uncensored me within these short autobiographical prose acting as titles for the poems in this collection.

Brief & Bleeding Margins

Bloody
POLITICS

When You Didn't Tell Anyone Your Opinions For A Long Time Then One Day You Admit To Yourself That You're A Feminist And, For The Most Part, You Actually Hate America. After Reading Poems by Jericho Brown, You Suddenly Have A Lot To Say And You're Happy You Only Sacrificed A Husband For Your Voice.

Just tell yourself you'll do something. Then tell someone else. Or don't because that's up to you. But all the while, *you're actually doing it.* It being...

Sshhhhh

Patriarchy is a roach motel. Guests itch—let's be honest: we all itch. That creeping across your dishes is a certain kind of taste & sound. *You can even hear it now, maybe even on your tongue.* They can't be killed but you'll be charged for every second they're alive. An infestation always starts with a single scurry. An obligation & an era of feminine oppression for the sake of procreation is handed out on twitching antennae. A never-ending epoch of subjugation—just wearing different boots & glasses, different heels & hats. These are all the diseases roaches carry...

Sshhhhh

Capitalism eats rotting meat off the bone. You can hear the roar of a lion: crunching—slinking up the staircase of debt. Like a sphynx—*stocking* before it pounces. Don't ask me where my money really is. It's all paper & bones. & by paper I mean trees. I mean green. I mean...I'm broke. By bones I mean...bones in my brain. Bones in the dirt. Bones. Paper roots wrapping around bones in the dirt—in the brain. Capitalism is actually a skeleton. You ever wonder how many times there's a real purr before the bite? A lion roars because there is always a bite just before...

Sshhhhh

Homophobia is a snake in a hole. Or *maybe* not. It could be a snake in a field of high wheat & wind. Or maybe it doesn't matter where the snake is. It's going to lay in hiding. Weaving in & out of patriarchy & wrapped around capitalism. This snake wants to tempt & wrongfully accuse gay, trans, and drag. But it's your slinking fear—the real slithering serpent. Wherever the snake is, it's going to shed its skin on everything. Everything being...

Sshhhhh

Rest in Peace: to sleep, perchance an American dream or a waking nightmare. Rest in Pieces: a puzzle of neurons, cosmos, thought. Our broadcast News is a lack of information. Our newsfeed is a lack of inhibition. We're all moving at the speed of sound. All put in the ground. Or left to float in the sky, learning to fly higher than our false ideals. We all rest eventually but why is it only after moving between tired & really *fucking* tired that we see the truth? I'll just be over here French kissing my own survival before eating lunch with radical acceptance. With or without heaven...

Sshhhhh

When *#PinkTax* Trended On Social Media To Help *People* Who Bleed Monthly Thanks To That New York Times Article About Putting The Word "Tampons" On A Ballot Finally But They Still Don't Want *Them* In A Man's Bathroom. And Somehow Everyone Got Distracted With "Men's Razors" Being Better Than Women's. But A Blade Is Made To Cut No Matter What Kind Of Skin The Hair Grows From. So, We Wait…Wait For True Equal Rights…For ALL.

Pink, like my insides—the softest, warmest part.

What's with that extra 2% charge for tampons & pink razors?
Fuck the pink pens & pink bubble gum
& the pink…pink…pink…   *Fuck.*

I didn't even chew that gum but sure, charge me
as I stretch off the bottom of your shoe.

I make 17% less than a man—maybe more.
Maybe less. I don't know…I just go off bar graphs
& I'm supposed to be grateful
there's a pad dispenser in the bathroom?

I bitch about $1 for a "thick & long" like I'm bleeding out
my entire uterus in one foul swoop of goop.
But that pad is *ALSO* a privilege.
So, why are we still on with the *His* & *Hers* bullshit anyway?

Do you want us *in* a diaper
or do you want us to *change* them?
To you, I should just be someone's mother.
Blind eyes to the former brothers.

Hello, ballot. Goodbye, patriarchy…*Just kidding…*
That fight still goes on monthly—no matter how the body identifies.

Pink tax is another charge for our existence:
a marketing ploy on our vaginas.

But here's my middle finger in the form of a Diva Cup.
A *fuck you* with the perfect *pop* every time I pull it out.
This rubber cone is a red Queen's crown.

This one-time diva fee
got me feeling like a bleeding victor.
If I still had a pink string to tug
I would rip out the bloodiest part of me.

& smear it across this bullshit Pink Tax.

When Politicians Use Glory Holes Then Hold The Floor, Canceling Drag Shows Instead of Guns. Only After Writing Bills That Take Away Rights Instead of Punishing Rapists. And You're Just So Sick Of White-Cis-Men Having The Last Word, So You Write A Pissed-Off Poem About It.

I whisper into tampons
& toilet paper rolls
stacked in the trash bin—

I want to know…
what's the end game?

You've got ink in my womb.
Drafting—wait, scratch that—
eradicating laws.

You need to tell me…
for what?

To swing your power like a sword?
To pretend you're not just a pencil stuffed
through a rusty hole in the wall?

I want to know…
for what?

To show me I don't deserve my power?
Like I'm not worth the toxic cotton
or the bubblegum pink plastic that holds it:

These tools we hide
in our palms
on the way to the bathroom every month.

Anything is a weapon...
if you hold it just right.

You scribble my number onto the stall.
Only it's not for a good time—
it's for a lifetime.

If it's a felony to abort
then is the end game to erase my vote?

That's how you'll legitimize my disappearance.
I'll become rubber dust brushed
& dumped into the trash.

I want to know...
what's the end game?

My number fossilizes on the stall.
But what about the baby?
Will you still demand it born...

if in time, *he* adds an *S* & a *dress*?
How can you give them your middle finger
while holding the Bible?

Is your goal to keep books
off their shelves?
Oh, it's the fear you must feel

if they dog-ear the right side of history.
Your ink-stained fingers
leave prints around their necks.

You need to tell me...
for what?

Is it all for larger prison populations?
For free labor—to put toilet scrubbers
in incarcerated hands?

Who will paint over & over
& over the bathroom stall until
my number becomes invisible?

Preschools fester muses.
Are you afraid prisons will too?

My womb is not an incubator.
It's not here to populate either.
Not for you.

When 30,000 Feet In The Sky Becomes A Women's March For Equal Rights Then Your Feet Hit The Ground. But You're Just Trying To Raise Good Humans Who Don't Treat Other Humans Like Less Because It's Still A World Where Somehow That Doesn't Always Happen.

30,000 feet in the sky
with MSNBC silent on the seat in front of me.
Frantic & alone, ears buzz through the altitude.
A man next to me smiles as he watches FOX News.

Roe vs. Wade was reversed today.
My right to choose what *my* body does
or does not grow.
Striped away by five people in robes.

How much longer until I don't have the right
to move through the world without permission?
Until I release my children—
throwing them onto native dirt
to navigate a new theological America?

We're not a God-fearing family.

My children equate laws with morals
& that's my burden to unteach—
to rewire a connection they're taught in school.
In an America that doesn't want them to learn history
so that *rewind* button can always be pushed:
misogyny & hate on repeat.

Feminism can be a religion, *right?*

The plane lands.
I want to know if 34A or 19B
lifting their luggage from overhead
hurt with me.
Does 20C carry bags heavier with fear now
that our feet are on the ground?

I want to know if 28A or 6B will help women
take our steps back. By *back,* I mean
to be *our own* again. *To have* again.

Will 27C help women take steps forward?
We've only got 30,000 or so feet to go.

When Your Lifelong Best Friend Struggles To Get Pregnant And You Give So Much Support You Even Offer To Be A Surrogate But Instead, They Use Other Science And You're Hopeful For Her Because She Deserves To Build Her Family In The Way She Wants. Yet You're So Fucking Mad That The Government Keeps Stripping Down Every Right For A Woman To Choose. You Know The Literal Pain Of Birth And You See Her Pain For Not Knowing. You Also Know The Pain Of Women Identifying People Getting Their Hands Tied. Every Kind Of Woman And Her Controlled Hormones. Controlled Pain. Pain In Their Bodies…Their Bodies Losing Battles On All Fronts. So, You Just Write A Satire Poem About This Painful World That Women Really Should Be Running By Now. I Mean After All, If They Can Handle Cramps And Childbirth, They Can Handle The World's Problems.

The GOP Rep from Texas said, *"Watch a sonogram of a 15-week-old baby... if they're a male baby they may have their hand between their legs...if they feel pleasure, why is it so hard to believe they feel pain?"* Because why not think in utero masturbation is more important than the woman housing the waterbed he is cradled in?

It's the only form of self-pleasure God accepts. After the baby is born, he'll wear mittens to break the habit. I mean mittens protect his face from those God-given fingernails. I mean, masturbating is a sin.

> Forget the Mom who was raped because after all...

"Women don't get pregnant that often from rape," said the GOP Rep from Arizona. Because those soon-to-be-moms are probably lying anyway.

We must, above all, always protect the unborn men because, someday he'll grow up to get his brand-new wife pregnant. He'll never have to masturbate again. Because a wife's *only* purpose is to *please* her husband, right? I mean, he'll break her in. I mean, masturbating is a sin.

> What if that masturbating baby in her womb hangs sequin clothes in his closet that look better on him than his wife? What if he grows up & adds an *S* to his pronoun?

Oh no, that's not going to happen. There's bans & bills for that. I mean there's separate bathrooms still. Don't forget, there's camps for that. If it fails, there's God to answer to. I mean, there's more than one sin.

> But why do men get to play God with a woman's body? A woman's right to choose?

Don't you know? It's because women don't masturbate.

The late-great Rush Limbaugh said, *"You know how to really stop an abortion? Require that each one occur with a gun."*

We surely do miss his truly righteous suggestions because most of them just make me want to get a gun.

When You Learn The Roe V. Wade Baby—The Baby Whose Mother Fought Her Way Up To The Supreme Court And Won The Right For Women To Choose. The Baby Whose Mother Was Still Forced To Give Birth To Her Because It Took More Than Nine Months To Gain This Freedom Is Neither Pro-Choice Nor Pro-Life And That's Not A Cop-Out. Shelley Lynn Thornton *Lives* With The Trauma of Being Born Truly *Unwanted* And Then Made Famous For It. So, All I Can Do To Process That Is Write A Haiku.

One woman, her womb:
forced birth leads to weary lives.
Women's Right To Choose.

When The Earth Sprouted Cotton And Then Cis White Men Abused Black People And Women And Brown People And Children For Hundreds And Hundreds Of Years And You Don't Know What To Do Except Write A Poem. Then You Spend Three Long Nights Reading About The Industrial Revolution And Early America After Skimming The Bills Slated For The Current Supreme Court. Sadly, It's All The Same Damn Shit. Let's Just Hope There's A Loud Enough Pen to Pick The Padlocks.

Cotton. Before it was toxic.
    Silhouettes in the sun.
        Flowers still plucked:
            wilting without water.

Cotton dresses (for her), trousers (for him)?
    Factories full of children
        with curls pulled from scalps.
            Rainbows on wooden floors:
                ruby splatters, splinters.

Cotton catches blood
    until it absorbs breast milk.
        Motherhood begins as a milking cow.

Cotton. Before pink plastic tubes.
    Fields of freckled faces:
        more hands to help, but more to feed.
            Dowries & dollars paid for one another.

History knows cotton.
    The *Earth* knows cotton.
        Men know cotton.
            Babies know cotton.
                Women know cotton.
                    The *body* knows cotton.
                        Her-story knows cotton.

*W*hen You Live In A "Click & Collect" World, So Amazon Trucks Roll Down Your Street Six Times A Day And You Feel Obligated To Wave, *Hello* To The Amazon Guy In The Next Lane At A Red Light Because, Hell, He Might Be The Guy Who Delivered Your Diva Cup Or The "Horny Honey" Cream You Needed To Get Through The Last Year Of Your Life. So, You Are Happy To Say, *Thank You* With A Little Smile And A Contrapuntal Poem Where It's Read Down The Left Column, The Right, Then Across—Something Similar To A Delivery Route.

Amazon has the *Also Bought*
feature turned on—
you buy in, keep buying.

Keep the supply chain going
with "Add to cart."
Add. Add. Add to cart.

Also Bot—
Window Shop Robot:
Amazon *Also Bought.*

Also Bot Robot—
Click, click, click
that little yellow button.

You may *also* like that
because they *also* bought this
so someone else may *also* buy it.

Keep shopping for an item
You might like it:
You *also* love it. Buy it.

Also Bot—
Window Shop Robot:
Amazon *Also Bought.*

Also Bought Robot:
Add to the cart.
Or save for later.

Also Bot—
Window Shop Robot:
Amazon *Also Bought.*

Amazon window shop:
Until your cart is over $100.
Also Bought Robot.

Also Bot Robot—
Click, click, click
that little yellow button.

Don't forget:
A new credit card.
You're pre-approved!

Also Bot—
Window Shop Robot:
Amazon *Also Bought.*

Also Bought Robot
keeps you buying.
Clicking that yellow button.

When The New York Times Keeps On With The Bad News But Sprinkles In A Good Book Review Every Once In A While, Except That's Not Good Enough Because $10K In Student Loan Relief Would Change Your Life. Instead, Another Bank Is Bailed Out And You're Still Vying For That Higher Paying Job With Health Insurance. So, In The Meantime You Read All The Articles And Hope You Won't Need To Go To The Doctor… Like, Ever. So, Here's A Pantoum For Debt.

For the 99%, debt is a lemon meringue pie.
It's yellowing & fluffy, like a political candidate.
Too tangy: this sweet a lie
bought & sold at a high interest rate.

Yellow & fearful—not like a political candidate—
I'm waking up to tragedy on the newsfeed.
Buy & sell us at a higher interest rate.
Wool over our eyes. Licking your lips with greed.

Waking to another tragedy. The news feed:
breadcrumbing a feel-good story…
hoping we'll take a bite. Sweet & flaky. *Just read.*
Ignoring the bloody truth in all its glory.

More breadcrumbing. A feel-good story
is too tangy. This sweet a lie
ignores the bloody truth. It's just gluttonous glory.
For the 1%, debt is not a lemon meringue pie.

EMERGING,

Briefly

When This Poem Was Supposed to Be About A Real Flower, But You Got A Paper Cut And Realized It Was About Origami. Then You Remember Losing Your Virginity And Realize This Poem Is Really About Rape. This Poem Wanted to Be A Haiku But It Still Came Out Like Origami Because That's What Poetry Does To You. So, Tell Me, What Does It Do For You? What Words Slice Through You? Is It Just Paper Or The Fear Of Hearing *No?* Because That's What Rape Culture Is.

Only, the world took me
as a delicate paper flower.
Expecting me to grow—
from seed to vase
without a thorn.

Prick-prickly fingers.
Pearls of blood
as they hold me too tightly
in their crushing palms.
Refolding me until the creases fit.

When Spring In Colorado Arrives And You're Still So Disgusted By Plums Because There Was So Much Throw Up From That Unsuspecting Rotten One You Ate When You were Seven But Your Kids Keep Requesting Them. All The While You're Still Hating Patriarchy, Dating Women For The First Time Since Freshman Year Of College, And You Keep Telling Yourself That Little Moments From Your Childhood Mean Little As An Adult So Your Kids Will Be Okay. But You Keep Having Metaphorical Memories.

When I was younger
I ate plums
all summer long.
Unrestricted juices
flowed over my lips
down my chin
intrepidly onto my dresses
already stained
green to match
the hills I rolled down.
I watched the world spin
with strawberry shortcake
underwear exposed.
The older boys
snickering.
On my face
a tender smile
meant to keep me company
on the way to my future.
Little did I know then
what could be used as collateral.
It only takes one acidic plum
to forever ruin
their appeal.

When You Remember Sears Is For Deals & Grooming Because You Began To Notice All The Closed Roebuck Stores On I-25 Between Denver And Fort Collins But All You Can Think About Is Your Empty Womb After Taking An Abortion Pill When You Were A Teenager. Even If You Don't Regret It, You Can Finally Admit You Need To Heal From It. Even When Your Two Kids Fight In The Back Seat, You Still Think About The Child You Were When You Made Such An Adult Choice.

1. *Roebuck In The Shoe Department*
Remember his first little fib? He said you stuck your hands in the high-end heels to make them dance. A fib designed to make you feel like a teen-twit—innocent & infantile. He controlled the security camera. Zooming in time & time again on your intentionally exposed thong, push-up bra pressing fresh cleavage strategically up. So, you let the fib sit on your skin.

2. *Roebuck With A Badge*
When a man carries a badge, you think there's a promise made to something greater than the sweet spots between your bodies, but he wears the slick & shiny metal like a mask. Remember the night in an empty parking lot, windows fogged over with Lolita lust? His security badge gleamed in the cop's flashlight as he pulled his driver's license from the wallet. You did the math quick: he's 29, not 21. Your newly-earned license, left in your bookbag. This man let off with a warning.

3. *Roebuck In Seedy Motels*
You're such an asshole for leaving a perfectly suitable sweet date at junior prom. But he was your age & he was nice & you left him to drive your shitty teal Ford Escort to a seedy little motel in the next town over. "What were you thinking?" Parents always ask. "You weren't," parents always answer their own question. *Maybe you weren't.* But you sat in the car reapplying eyeshadow & deodorant, perfuming the darkest parts of yourself, listening to 311's "Love Song." You drove home with smeared makeup, his sticky stench on your breasts. The radio turned off.

4. *Roebuck Before There Were Hashtags*
After your last narcissist, you can't help but ask, "Who was the first?" There's no one there to answer but yourself. Before #lovebomb #devaluestage #sexualabuse you still knew it was risky business even if you couldn't see the power dynamic in full slant. What kinds of mistakes do people make when they don't have anyone telling them what they're experiencing isn't normal? Someday, you'll be an expert on yourself if you keep looking in the mirror, keep asking the hard questions. Can anyone change the outcomes of a choice made when they didn't know what was right or wrong? No. That's what experience is for—it's what you get when you don't have it when you need it.

When You Yell At Your Kids For Eating Their Strawberry Shortcake Chapstick Then Remember You Did The Same When You Were Their Age. You Think "This Must Be Another Part Of Growing Up" Then You Go To The Bathroom To Cry On The Toilet Because You Hope Your Kids Treat The Person They *Take* Or *Lose* Their Virginity *To* Or *From* With More Respect Than You Experienced.

This can't be growing up.
Posture will always be in rebellion with stature:
permanent markers keep score
on door frames.

It's no longer Disneyland
or cotton candy.
It's no longer Kool-Aid
or dollhouses.

Grown-up Barbies
with lanky legs that blossom into secrets
that can't be kept—
can't be vindicated.
Can't be softened by the truth.

Skinned knees in short skirts.
No matter how much
strawberry shortcake lip gloss
she licks off her teeth.

She sleeps with a has-been Prince
on a bed without sheets
and wakes to find a slipper
flushed down the toilet.

When You Lived In Brooklyn For A Decade And Got So Used To Catcalls And Uninvited Sexual Advances On The Block That It Began To Feel Like An Open Field of Corn Swaying In The Heat Of July And Not A Scene From A Rom-Com Movie Set In New York. You Were Not So Naive Though; These Were The Beginning Days Of iTunes And Earbuds So You Avoided Technology Making You An ATM Or Another Kind Of Victim. But It Wasn't Until You Watched An Abduction Unfold Before Your Eyes At 3 AM On Myrtle And Waverly Ave. That You Vowed To *Always* Have Both Ears Open. Sadly, That Ensured You Heard All That "Ay Yo, Ma" Bullshit.

A beautiful woman and an ugly man stand on a corner at Barclay Center. They wait for the signal to walk.

The ugly man says, *A beautiful little woman here to be a model or an actress on the big screen? Can you sing me a song, the tune of your heart that will top the charts?*

I am the dirt under the feet of a diligent farmer. Trudging on me leaves the mark of his soul on my face. In my nose, he plants a seed.

The ugly man says, *A beautiful little woman, you should be up on that billboard, not the can of Pepsi. It should be your face on the television, not that news anchorman spewing lies.*

I am a corn stalk with ears that touch the sky. I will reach God today. *What is the meaning of life?* I ask him.

The ugly man says, *A beautiful little woman, you're not meant to walk, come home with me and I will lie you down on my bed. I will paint a picture of you, better than The Birth of Venus.*

The sun is setting, says the beautiful woman while looking up through the skyscrapers. The harvest moon will be out tonight. *And I will bleed on your sheets.*

When My College Roommate Fell In Love With A Gay Guy But It's A Happy* Ending Because Both Of Them Married Men. There's An Asterisk Because I Don't Keep In Touch With Either Person Except The Rare And Random Facebook Post. They're Always Grinning In Expensive Clothes So They Must Be Better Off…Probably…I Guess.

All starry-eyed, she giggles.
Pigtails & cigarettes.

With raunch & warming oils
parading around, vulgarly awkward.

Eyeliner & secrets—dark black & red
shared, like tampons.

More like best friends
with knives to each other's backs.

He tells her about blowjobs.
The ones she'll never give him.

Confusion lies silently in bed with them—
wrapped together like question marks.

When A Blow-Up Doll From Chuck Palahniuk Becomes A Metaphor For How Much You Love Your Best Friend But Don't Know How To Tell Her That You Might *Love-Love* Her And Not Just Love Her Like Platonic Love. So, You Write Love Poems Disguised As Appreciation Poems For Her.

My dad just died
so, I'm looking through a big ass tote
of mementos for his memorial.
Right under some blurry pictures
of clear memories is a blow-up doll.

A Barbie-type blow-up doll
with big tits & a wide mouth.

Rewind back to June, July *or maybe* August of 2008—
can't actually remember because the heat
in New York doesn't let up once it starts.
The stench of the city sits on everything—
that toxic *ooze* smell hits my knees
as I weave through the slow tourists
& asshole moneymen in lower Manhattan.

I lumber block after block with my backpack
full of every book Chuck published at that point—
each book snatched off my shelf
in hopes of adding his bleeding ink
to the title page when we finally meet.

It was hot as *hell*
but no one fainted during his reading—
from either *heat or shock*.

But he did bring those blow-up dolls—
the hot-air, naked-over-sized Barbie dolls
& tossed them out into the crowd.

Sam Rockwell showed up
wearing Air Force One basketball shorts
which, I guess, makes sense
since he was the star of the new movie
adaptation of *Choke*.

The audience was about that realness—
Chuck's not a staged kind of guy.
I think. & Sam *smelled* like New York
when he handed me a peach-toned ball
of plastic possibility.

I held the blow-up doll to my chest—
that sexy-sex-doll—like a prized Barbie.
& yes, he signed my entire backpack full of books.
Thank you.

For the next three years I tortured my roommate
with that not-so-sexy-life-size Barbie-doll.

No. Not like that.
Get your head out of…your head.

I would blow up that doll
& leave it outside of her door
tape it to the ceiling of her room
prop it up in the shower
during her insomniatic episodes.

My attempts at scaring her
resulted in serene walks out of her room
or lying down & peacefully closing her eyes
or just enjoying a steamed-up shower
covered in suds, unscathed.

Our walls were thin & my cackling laughter
at her imagined terror never did the trick.
It took some time, but I learned she was blind
without her contacts. *Ha*! Tricks are for fools.

I think about asking if she ever got-got
by my blow-up Barbie-doll traps
because, believe it or not
she's still my best friend.
She was the first person I called
after my dad died.

When You Begin Dating Again (Oh-So-Reluctantly) After A Thirteen Year Relationship Ends And You're Healed Enough To See Everything As A Giant, Waving, Red Flag. Then You Think Maybe It's You, That You're The Problem, So You Start Writing Down The Shit These Men Say And Realize It's Not You. You're Not The Problem.

I prefer long hair, you could just put extensions in.

You don't wear too much makeup, that's good. I don't like that shit on my pillow in the morning.

You have a nice smile, but it would look better if you wore red lipstick.

You should wear more dresses.

All boys should play sports. You need to sign up your boys for football or soccer.

Johnny Depp was the only victim—I'm glad he won.

I was falsely accused of sexual harassment three times.

You would be my prettiest friend with benefits.

I am an alpha male.

My ex is crazy.

My daughter will never date a Black guy.

A woman can't be President.

You should eat more.

You could do without desert.

Women are too sensitive.

When You've Seen The Tree Outside Your Bedroom Window Bloom And Die Twice Since The Last Time You Had Sex. Sometimes That Brings You Joy But Other Times You Look Out The Window And Your Mind Wanders To Sensualizing Non-Sensual Objects. Maybe You Really Do Feel Like You Might Actually Want to Be With Women. You're Just Letting Your Mind Reap Back To A Fruit You've Always Appreciated But Are Actually Attracted To. Or Maybe You're Just So Hungry. So. Damn. Hungry.

There's never been a more beautiful mango.
Equate it to finally hugging the tallest tree.

I'm not talking about a redwood here—
I'm talking about the roots inside my fingertips.

I'm talking about that crusty patch of dirt
that catches the right light any time of day.

I'm talking about looking up & seeing a tree so tall
That I (a lover of books) get mad at paper.

I've *never* held a more beautiful mango.
In all its orange & greens bleeding on skin—

so smooth I became Aphrodite in a costume contest.
Except, I only want the type of love that's true.

I'm pickier & more tired now.
I'm done working with just what's at hand.

It's not about *he/him* or *she/her*.
Is love a mango or a tree?

A tree with rings & rings...
a branch with leaves & leaves—

greens to reds:
all seasons breathe through me.

Give me juice or give me death.
I choose death.

No, not really. I choose the yellowing
meat hanging from the mango pit.

First, I'll need to plant a seed
from the best mango tree.

When You Read An Article About Discovering The First Calendar Of Mankind And It Was A Piece Of Leg Bone With 28 Notches Carved In A Jagged Line. The Author's Question Stands Out In the Middle Of the Page: "What [Cis]Man Needs to Make A 28 Day Calendar?" And Maybe People Who Read That Article Will Realize More Credit Needs To Be Given To Those Who Bleed.

I was on birth control for nearly a decade
before finally letting my body sync
with its own 28-day calendar.

I broke up with my boyfriend
then told myself being free of the birth control
would ensure my celibacy.

Only I welcomed that man back into my bed
on a pitch-black night.

It was only 52 days
until I was told I was pregnant
in the gynecologist office.

Wouldn'tcha know...
during a birth control
reinstatement appointment.

Flash-forward through many cycles:
astrological & abusive.

Through 18 months of pregnancy.
Through 42 months of nursing.
Through 36 months of Nexplanon.

Finally, his vasectomy.
I'm free of the pill again
and I'm finally free from him.

I kicked him out of my bed—
out of my life on another pitch-black night.

Now I follow the moon—
making notes in my digital calendar
on the first day I bleed each month.

15 cycles celibate now.
420 days on my own bones.
In case you're counting.

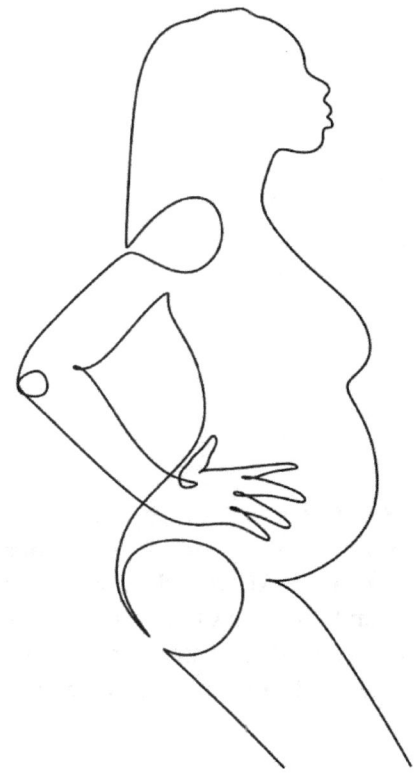

MOTHER'S
Blood

When Your R.E.M Cycle Is Interrupted For A Decade Because You're A Mother Even When You're Asleep. But When You Become A Single Mom, You Learn About The Tortured Glory Of Alone. You Become Your Own Body Again After You Aren't Mad At The Loneliness Because There's A Lot Less Tears In The House Even If There's No Sex. But You Start Masturbating For The First Time In Your Life, Without Shame.

I lie awhile then we're the same height:
my hips fit into the space
between mattress & wall.
I whisper into the sheets:

I want *you* to be my speed & light.
You end up being fast
& slow down. Enjoy my company.
My own, alone.

When I lie quite awhile
you hold me like an origami flower.
You never disappoint me
by being *you*: my own, alone.

My hands grope for *you*.
Freed from the night
when I wake in the morning glow—
alone, but my own.

I ask if *you* slept well.
The translation is
that I am love with *you*
no matter the answer.

I see *you* & I am satisfied.
I see *you* & I dilate.
Every poem has a "you."
A *you* the poet writes to.

& *I'm* it.
I am my own, *alone*.

When You Were Married To A Man Who Is Only Good At Cooking, So You Gain More Weight During Covid Than You Did During Both Your Pregnancies. All The While, Becoming Obsessed With Celebrities On Social Media Because You Hate Yourself So Much. Then You Write A Poem Called, "Sexy Me Poem" Late At Night For All The Sad People Of The World Who Struggle With The High And Low Numbers On Their Scales. For All The Sad People Of The World Who Struggle With Comparing Themselves To Other Sad People Who Are Just Having A Hard Time Falling Asleep With A Cell Phone Light In Their Face, Just Like You.

Look at sexy me with sexy lips puffed and sexy red Look at me in my sexy skinny skinny jeans sexy Look at me with my sexy toes stuffed in my sexy peek-a-boo sexy black heels Look at me all sexy and sex Look at me in sexy high-def Look at me on sexy glossed magazine covers Look at sexy me sexing up the internet Look at sexy me sexier than you Sexy sex oozes from my sexy vagina Sexy sex bleeds from my sexy cuts Look at sexy me with my sexy ass on the dance floor.

When Your Ex-Mother-In-Law Buys You A 23andMe Kit But All The Results Tell You Is You're *Fucking White* And You Don't Know How To Look In The Mirror Because You Know That Most Of Your Ancestors Were Probably On The Wrong Side Of History. So, You Tell Yourself You'll Break The Cycle For Your Kids But You Realize That Half Their Grandparents Are Alive And You're Mad That They're Not Willing To Start Making Your Ancestors Angry Too.

We talk about being on the wrong side of history like it doesn't start with family. Like there's no families without fathers. *So selfish & blind.* Like there's no families with mothers boiling in the shower until their skin is red because that's the only time it's really quiet. Like there's no space between sadness & fear.

We talk about being on the wrong side of history like it doesn't start with ancestry. Passion isn't just for Italians. Big teeth aren't just for Norwegians. Some people in England are okay with microwaving their tea. Even some of the Polish population is allergic to sour cream.

We talk about being on the wrong side of history like it doesn't start with family. Like a Grandmother *must* stand by her son when he abandons his kids. Like a Grandfather shouldn't stand up for his daughter even though he walks with a cane. Like brothers can't be scared to sleep alone when they've only ever known sharing a room. Why can't I just cry in my car? In the bathroom at work, or at the grocery store?

We talk about being on the wrong side of history like it doesn't start with family.

When You're Beyond House Poor Because You Promised Your Kids That You Would Do Whatever It Took To Keep Their Home After Your Divorce And Of Course Everything Starts Falling Apart Just As You're Getting Your Life Together. But You Can't Afford To Fix Anything And The Worst Of It Is The Jackhammer Of A Man Who Left Everything Broken.

Slabs of stones, uneven & broken, fit together
to make a path around our home.

The drilling shakes the windows & dust crusts
in the creases of his hands, under his fingernails.

The cracks in our walls start small:
etch-a-sketch scratches form in the back

then advance through the kitchen, up the stairs
crisscross ceilings & down the front wall.

I trace them daily—marking their distance
to memory.

It was the demolition of cement under those slabs.
It was digging out the foundation.

Leaving gnarly & ever-connecting
fractures through our home.

There's a canyon in the door. Not from our broken base.
But his foot.

No escape from the jackhammer of a man
who left us with paths of destruction.

A crumbling rumble—all that remains is a pile
of limbs & drywall.

We shackle the cracks but there's no hope yet
of patching ourselves into wholeness again.

When Death Is A Mushroom Or Maybe It's Actually Healing. Or Maybe It's Just A Mushroom That Survives Like A Mother Who Digs Herself Out After Divorce. A Mother Is A Mushroom And If You're Not Sure How, Just Ask A Single One. She Will Tell You Through Her Angered or Labored Breath. Through The Breath She Holds For Her Children While Trying To Enrich Their Soil.

From root & stem to a full-blown, slime-covered cap. *Poison* or *shaved truffle?* Standing. Silent, unseen. Growing in the dark, eating the dead of the Earth.　　　　　　Slowly.

A mushroom *cannot* be existential.

Maybe I'm the decomposing matter feeding fungus. Still clinging to what I once was. Aching to live.

My fur forfeits into patches thanks to oxygen—what gave life now melts my insides, oozing into soil. Losing myself in the stench of the unknown. I soak into the skin of worms who know only dirt—the path they dig,
　　　without sight.

Maybe I'm the worm. No legs & an invisible heart that beats only to feast on humus—my sulfur sorrow. Road maps in the nutrients mushrooms make.

I might be the lingering moist smell after death has cleared & morning light desiccates blood & dew. Just before the sun casts its harsh heat & shrivels creatures that thrive in the dark. The mushroom will finish its job: to grow through　　　　　death.

All that's left is a thick moss in my leaf-littered forest. Maggots fester before they fly, bones & fibers　　　　descend.

I burrow my way to the surface only to find myself on a hook & so far from my already segmented existence. Into the mouth of a trout: wide-eyed & gasping in the air that will kill it.

So, *maybe* I'm the porcelain dish warmed by truffles & fish—fried crisp with burnt butter & crust made from bread that could only bake with wheat from fertilized soil.

Did I forget yeast? A mushroom's distant friend. Always eager to meet & kiss the air. So, *maybe* I'm the stomach that stretches full after the last bite. Or maybe always　　　just a
　　　　　　　mushroom.

When Your Children's Father Left You All For His Own Fun And You've Got Big Ass Things To Worry About, Like Mental Health For Three, Like Filling Their Two Bellies Before Your One. And The Nights That Go On And On For A Few Months With Your Kids Sleeping In Your Bed Because Their Abandonment Issues Manifest, Just As Expected. So, You Say *Fuck The Yard* And Give Yourself Grace To Work On Healing The Home, Formally Four. And You Say *Fuck The Father Too.*

I let the lawn burn to a crisp corn yellow with lush green bean-colored weeds sprouting around like bouquets of disgraceful hope. Grass isn't meant to grow in this Denver desert, definitely not this summer. I don't care what the neighbors think of my harsh yard. I'm conserving water with my rebellion: I've given myself the power to let go. To redirect my ambition & raging orange fire inside.

Or this lawn is just my mind—all dried up & tired. Drudging through the mud of our freshly broken family is harder than being barefoot among the curling & spiny weeds. I don't mind my lack-of-lawn because my children have shattered hearts & I'm trying to mend this cracked home. The water is just wasted on this non-grass. We need it to wash our skin, our clothes, & dishes. We need it to wash our souls, to calm our insides, to cool our stomachs from the aches that seep down from our chests. I'm not wasting my time with any other seedlings this season. I've got to water my children. My healing keeps flooding our house so, I've got nothing left for the lawn.

My children don't feel shamed by the dusty chocolate yard because toy swords are scattered & stabbed into crusted earth—ready for their next battle. They don't mind the rare blades of grass mixed with milkweed that scratch their knees when they fall because I wrap them in my arms when they get up.

This yellowing of the lawn gives way to dust rising around their feet as they act out dragon wars. Weeds are whacked over and over while they save imaginary villages from demons. A triumphant sun casts shadows—larger than life across the barren landscape of the dream world in their front yard. Afterall, they're escaping from the pain of our broken home too. At least they can conquer the lawn as they please.

When You Post A Facebook Status About Eating All Your Kids' Candy, Buying More For Them, Then Eating That Candy Too Because You're On Your Period And That's The Only Time You Crave Sugar Over Salt Then Someone Who Met You When You Were Underweight Comments That She Figured You For The Type Of Mom Who Would Only Have "Fruit & Nuts" For Snacks. It Doesn't Bother You At First. Then It Does Bother You. You Were Only Underweight Because You Didn't Have Enough Money To Feed Yourself And Your Kids That First Summer You Were A Single Mom. You Went Hungry So Your Kids Could Have Seconds. Maybe You're Not Bothered By The Misconception Of You As Much As You're Bothered By All The Misconceptions Of People And Their Bodies And You're Thankful You Never Had Body Dysmorphia Or An Eating Disorder But You Just Want To Hug Every Person Who Suffers From Either.

I can eat again: for mind, body, & heart.
Food for thought
is really knowing that I *don't* know
but have the hunger to learn.

I eat apples
even though I end up with cores.
Even if dappled skin slices my gums.

Fill my soul, emancipate my tastebuds.
I can't think of a food I don't like.
I graze on words & dip my ambition in chocolate
like begging my children to finish their dinner.

They want to know what's for breakfast at bedtime.
I kiss them on their cheeks, wish them fruitful dreams
about all the sweet things they hope for:

>   —salted caramel—
>   —fresh pretzels—
>   —straws that flavor milk—
>   —raspberries from our neighbor's yard—

Sleep is their secret space to feel & grow.
I go into their room to watch their mouths:
open, drying through the night.

I spy candy wrappers under their pillows.
I smile.
Then move the candy box to a higher cabinet.

When Motherhood Is A Pie But If The Crust Burns Just Use A Butter Knife To Scrape Off The Dark Spots Because It'll Still Taste Good.

1. Melt ½ cup butter then fold in chopped windows of time.

2. Set oven to 300 degrees, make the same requests over & over until your temple is as hot as the oven:
   Pick up your socks.
   Flush the toilet.
   Please brush your teeth.

3. Slowly whisk in 1 cup flour, 1 tbsp baking soda, ½ cup Legos and a million questions:
   Mommy, would you still love me if I bit you?
   Mommy, what's for dinner?
   Mommy, can I have candy?

4. Add an egg & an extra 15 minutes to every task in your day:
   Packing lunches.
   Getting out the door (forget about on time).
   Mommy, are you mad I broke your favorite coffee mug?
   Cleaning the bathroom.
   Taking your first shower in three days.
   Mommy, how do lizard tails grow back?

5. Stir ¼ cup sugar into being happier without a husband. Even if it's a different kind of hard.
   Repeat number 2.

6. After their bedtime, take a long breath & pour in a big glass of wine.
   Mommy, why do we have dreams?

7. Boil tears & snot-soaked tissues with a pinch of salt.
   If one child gets sick, you're sick. Sore throats & fevered foreheads spread as your bed fills with bodies through the night.
   Be sure your pajamas are warm. They'll steal your covers.

8. Bake for 45 minutes but stay up all night regretting every moment you raised your voice today—justified or not. Hope you'll wake early enough to forecast better resolutions for tomorrow.
   Mommy, are you awake?

When Learning To */rip/* Paper Is A Metaphor For Being A Mother But You're Also A Teacher, A Writer, A Woman Who Holds Pain Like A Pen Running Out Of Ink. You're A Woman Who Remembers Too Much But Still Doesn't Know Enough. You're Just Trying To Heal Quickly So Not To Give Your Kids Too Much Trauma.

I must not have known how to /rip/ paper into strips
when my mother found that letter I wrote to myself.
The hate scribbled in crayon with its mixed-up *b's* and *d's*.

An ironic sun in the top left corner
with rays of long waxy-wavey lines shining through:
"You'll never find a real frien-b."

But my mother knew it said "friend"
& she blamed herself.
Maybe it was the tears streaming down my face
like crisp /rips/ in notebooks for years to come.

/Ripped/ from beds, moved in & out of states across America.
I didn't have space in my mind to carry a memory
of learning to break apart paper.

I learned to keep myself together in all the other ways.
There were new tools:
        My smile *but only* as a weapon.
        My brain *but only* undercover.
        My heart *but only* in a box.
            Scissors.

The internet hit the mail with AOL CDs
& I could /*rip*/ on someone with my fingers
in a whole new way or I could get my heart /*ripped*/ out
by a message aging back to hieroglyphics.

Symbols had my mind racing.
Too many times, I sat, spinning in a chair
with a cat catching birds between my legs—

wondering how that away message could stay for so long
because, surely by now, the phone should have been picked up.
The connected cables between worlds, /*ripped/*.

I taught my kids to /*rip*/ for fun:
told them fingers are friends
going on a short walk down the page.

They're so gracious, these finger friends:
they wait for each other.
With each step forward the other catches up.

Somehow the /*rips*/ running down
their lives are clean enough
to always get taped back together.

There's a stack of paper next to my bed.
My nimble fingers make hearts in the dark.
Pointers & thumbs sometimes meet for a kiss.

Then I wake, ready to paste
each misshapen heart onto my nose.
My hands form a mask.

Today, I'm more than a frien-b to my own tears.
It takes time to become the glue that sticks my /*ripped*/ pieces
into a new masterpiece.

Most times it's not putting the puzzle papers back
in order, it's *piecing* a whole new story together.
It's those jagged half-sentences
& extra S's that make up how it *really ends*.

When Your Second Child Wasn't Hard On Your Body The Same Way Your First Was. There Wasn't An Extra 50 Pounds, No Swollen Nose, No Carpal Tunnel, Or A Broken Tailbone. But There Was The Worry Over His Chromosome Disorder And The Stress To Work Until You Gave Birth And Now All Your Fears Over That Extra Y In His XY Genes Are Coming True. You Still Hold Him Even When He Triggers All Your Trauma, Even When You're Still Not Healed Enough To Help Him. You Let Yourself Melt Into A Mother-Puddle When He Sees You Need A Hug Too And You're Grateful He's Brave Enough To Just Give It.

First my belly
        then my heart:
                cradled in cold, sweaty palms.

Little rages of red
        spark through blue eyes.
Screams shatter the floor like fists
        that bang on the walls
                of my womb.

Only two & I worry
        over his words.
                R's don't roll
                L's linger too long on his tongue.
                Waves rumble
                out with his W's.

Only five & he throws chairs
        at my head. Strength
                fueled by tongue-tied words.

Our tears
        soak the pages
                as I read him book after book.
Failing to regulate our breath.

Only seven & he's ripped
        his glass heart
                out of a wild sea of mood swings.
        He's a salt-stained message
torn from the bottle.

As hard as he breaks—
        as deep as his shards cut
he's still a Band-Aid of affection
        that wraps tightly over wounds.

Our skin seals
        in scarred kisses.
                We share wounds by now.

An unconditional kid
        filled to the brim
                with growling *I love you's*
                      & extra chromosomes.

That extra Y in exclamation marks.
        Pointed fingers
        clenched teeth
        screeching
        & feet stomping.

How does his love
      come in equal forms
            of too tight
               & so far away?
Why does his rage
      bubble over
            into crushing aches for hugs?

I'm scared.
      Trying to remember
            frontal lobe facts
            remember being young
            remember being the second sibling.

I'm scared
      about my inability
            to save him.
     About broken homes
           & an absent father.

I'm trying
      to remember
            grace.
But my baby
      is so damn
            angry.

When Your Oldest Child Declares *He* **Will Be A** *They* **And Their Therapist Says,** *"It's A Reaction To A Stifled Ability To Express Emotions For Most Of Their Life Because Their Dad Never Let Them Have Feelings."* **But You've Known Since Before They Could Talk That They Could Hold A Color Or Two On The Rainbow Flag, So It's Your Job To Say,** *"Okay,"* **To Say,** *"They/Them."* **It's Your Job To Keep Raising Them With Radical Acceptance In A World That Is Everything But. To Keep Raising Them To Be Themselves, Despite.**

I was asked
if I would let my sons
accept their child
being aborted.

I said
I would
only be ashamed
if they tried to push
their own will on a woman.

I was asked
if I would let my oldest
piss in a litter box
if he identified as a cat.

I said,
"Calm the fuck down.
It's just grammar to you
but it's existence
to THEM."

When Cavities Are A Rite Of Passage But Your Mom Got Mad When You Posted This Poem On Social Media Because She Felt Like She Was Made Out To Be A Bad Guy So, You Change The Title To This Title And She Might Be More Mad Now. She's Not The Bad Guy In Either Version Though Because There Is No Metaphor. She Was Just A Mom Making Sure Your Teeth Didn't Rot Out Of Your Head.

You made your way through my mouth,
happily befriending
chocolate, soda pop, & Fruit Roll-Ups.
Marking your territory—
trenches in my baby teeth.

My mother stood
behind me with a toothbrush.
General of the army—
fighting a war against you.
Fluoride, whitening, tartar control—
she wanted them all,
you resisted each!

I cried when you were found.
Novocain shots
brought tears
& made my feet jump
to attention.
You won the battle
when I lost the rotten tooth
to the earnest dentist.

You learned to love
the silver lining &
I learned to brush my teeth.

*W*hen You Give Yourself A Stick 'N' Poke Tattoo In Honor Of Your Dad Who Died In 2020 (But Not From Covid) Then You Call Your Brother At 3 AM And Read The Elegy You Wrote For Your Dad Just To Hear Someone Else Cry Over Someone You Never Knew How To Love Fully Until He Was Gone. At First, You Think, *Isn't That What Brothers Are For?* But You Instantly Hope For Your Brother's Healthy Grieving Because You Realize His Tears Were Because He Hasn't Begun Healing Yet.

On my forearm, tiny dots are poked one at a time. Slowly forming your name, except crooked like your teeth. Your name was my name, but it feels like only your son's name now. Like only his daughters' name—until it's not their name anymore either. My hand trembles. Sticking an ink-dipped needle into skin at a slight angle. - - - - It's genetic. Crooked teeth.

There's a photo of us in my desk drawer. You're probably around 26, bent over my chubby baby body wrapped in a white towel on a bed. I don't have any teeth yet—that's my age. You must have just taken me from the bath & mom must have felt some sort of love at that moment. A love that I never witnessed, but there it is, proof of love in my drawer. In another photo, time rewound tightly back to you at seventeen. You're casually sitting in a chair—one hand resting on your knee—so relaxed & ready for your life to start. A smile without any shame of your teeth. Tucked away in my memory box is a photo of me with that same smile.

Your name: a single loop & so many sets of parallel lines. I remember standing on my tippy-toes, next to your studio desk, watching you work, then rubber eraser dust getting into my eyes. You wiped my face—graphite smudges on my cheeks & nose—smeared and smiling. Matching teeth. You were a man of your hands: an artist, a builder, a rebuilder. Your name still lives on half a century's worth of paintings & sketches. Even after you lost your pinky finger, that name stayed the same—only the numbers at the end, growing larger with each year that passed.

On your deathbed, calloused hands, limp in mine. There were needles in your arms—no ink, just tubes connecting you to a life that you couldn't build or rebuild anymore. I leaned over you, but no one was there to witness my love. No one else there to capture it & save it in a drawer. You, wrapped in white blankets. You, & your crooked teeth. Me, saying the only other name you ever heard besides your given: *Dad*. And here I am, with all my fingers & no father. Just your crooked & blown-out name, now permanent on my arm. In all its sorrow & honor.

I cleaned out your studio, brushed the eraser dust off the desk, & put away your pencils. Tucked in one of your old sketchbooks, I found the photo of me where we shared the same smile—-the same school photo from my own memory box. But on the back, in my little girl handwriting I wrote your name twice. Then my graphite-soaked fingers smeared tears across my cheeks. I mimicked your signature nearly perfectly at ten but got it wrong on my arm at after you were gone.

When You Write A Poem For Dave Grohl After The Poem, *Dear Boy George* By Amy Gerstler Over The Course Of Fifteen Years And Then Read It At An Open Mic Because You Think It's Not As Heavy As The Poem About Your Dead Dad & Tattoos But You Cry Anyway Because All Of a Sudden You Realize You're Worried About Your Kids Growing Up To Be Like Their Emotionally Absent Father, Plus, You Were Really Depressed Through Most Of Your Marriage—Not Just Fighting The Depression Like You Had Assumed For So Long, So The Poem Punches You In Your Own Damn Face And You're Still Crying With Snot On Your Sleeve When Someone Comes Up To You After And Thanks You For Your Vulnerability. Then You Feel Like A Real Fucking Poet.

When I was younger, I had a weakness for musicians with tattoos, cheesy smiles, & songs that enhanced whatever mood I was in. You, you made me so weak I would just lie in bed all day listening to your voice, looking at that picture of you. You know the one. The one where you're wearing a "Virginia is for LOVERS" T-shirt.

You played the drums with Nirvana, & when you made a comeback as the lead singer & guitar player for Foo Fighters, I was actually happy Kurt was out of the picture. *I'm sorry*...I know he was your friend, but that band would have died if he didn't. Oh, that sounds terrible! I'm *not* a monster. I've lost friends to suicide too, some even while listening to Nirvana, so you must forgive me. But, anyway, Foo Fighters have insane lasting power. The kind you deserve. I really do think of you as the true survivor of the grunge era.

I could have married you. I would have cooked your dinner & helped you write lyrics before band practice. When I saw you in concert twenty years ago, you stopped in the middle of *Generator* & said, "Hey! Give that girl her shirt back...it looks like she wants it," then you went right back into singing, "Yeah...can't you hear my motored heart?" I was that girl! I did want my shirt back! See, you were looking out for me.

You were there for me—all through Covid isolation, with new music videos & benefit concerts in empty venues. After two hours, you said, "Hell, let's play one more...you're stuck on the couch anyway," then your guitar started playing *Everlong*. I was stuck on my couch & I had been waiting for you *too*.

Now, when I have a bad day, I take you (& my sons) to the car wash. I splurge on the rainbow soap & blast *Best of You* while eating a popsicle. I bang my head & air drum, then turn toward them in the back seat & in a terrifying calm state of motion & suspension, I scream, "I'll never give in!"

I must confess, for a long time, I wanted my children to love you as much as I do. But I've got to tell you, now, I really just hope they love me as much as you love your mom because *Virginia Is For Lovers*.

When Your Husband Has An Affair And You Lean Into Your Ability To Be A Night Owl Creative And An Early Bird Mom Because You Kicked Him Out Of The House And Want to Write A Million Poems About Healing But You Also Need To Take Care Of Everything Else In Your Life, And Your Kids' Lives, And Yet Sometimes Still Some Of His Life…All The Time. So, You Just Put Your Anxiety On The Page.

Mornings are my addiction.
    It could be worse.

The sun hits my face.
Goose-pimpled skin warms to life.

Orange glows on my lids—
remnants of last night's sunset.

Nights are my vice.
    It could also be better.

The moon shocks my spine
chilling my breath to near-death.

Tumult lingers in my hands—
false love voids our last touch.

I crave & loathe the morning light.
I loathe & crave the quiet night.

Brief

META-POSEY

When You Curse Your Muse Because It's Late At Night When You Mixed Up The Definitions For *Epigraph* & *Epigram* And You Just Want To Write So You Eat Half A Gummy Because You Live In Colorado But All You Get Is This Poem.

Epigraph: *A short quotation or saying at the beginning of a book or chapter, intended to suggest its theme.*

Epigram: *Pithy or saying expressing an idea in a clever and amusing way.*

Interruptions become wealthy without my muse.

I go to a coffee shop, but my muse is no caffé mocha grande.

The muse feasts on philosophy & eggs. I choke on crow.

If I don't exist by lunch, all is not lost if my muse cries for me.

I dog-ear pages when Shakespeare muses over love, yet there is Macbeth.

The news says, "Preschools fester muses" but so do prisons.

That re(re)-run is on: will I miss the muse?

My declining mind applies lipstick—my muse licks it off.

A muse is male & just as importantly, female.

Or maybe, my muse waits for me too in a genderless bathroom.

I want love letters to arrive but my muse can't find the postage stamp.

If my muse makes dinner, we will eat grilled cheese & drink wine.

The fan oscillates: *no…no…no.* But still cools the room for my muse.

All I can say is *fuck you, muse* as the fly strip waves in the wind.

9pm, 11pm, 1am—my mind's all cooped up. Muse, let's go masturbate.

Lotion softens the hands of my muse & the clock keeps ticking.

I sweat with my muse: we are wrapped now, together.

My muse is invisible like monsters—they both live in my closet.

Even with the dreaded *suddenly…*
muses sing after the cursor: words…form…like magic…
My muse is a midnight night owl.

When Insomnia Sits On Your Eyelids Because You've Been Writing This Same Damn Poem for 20 Years. Luckily, There Are So Many Pieces Of It In Every Poem That Has Ever Lived On Your Skin But You Can't Let It Go Because That Means Giving Too Much Of Yourself To The World. Yet, Looking Back You Wonder How You Wrote A Poem For Yourself That Hits Like A Viral Tik-Tok Before The Internet Lost The Sound Of Dial-Up. You Look Back On Yourself Now And Wonder If You Could Have Known Then What You Know Now, Would You Have Made The Same Mistakes? All You Can Do Is Teach Your Kids Accountability, Teach Them Accidents Don't Mean Shame, Teach Them To Not Just Say *Sorry* But To Actually Learn From Their Mistakes.

My face gleams blue at night. Scrolling on—reading between the lines. Life is the marks in the margins, the scratches & swirls we make when trying to get the pen to work again. I can't remember waking up and my life not looking like cream in black coffee before we stir. Looking more like a negative exposure of the cup. Secretly, I want to be the lipstick painting the brim.

Why don't I carry change anymore? Even though change is the only constant. Time feels like a cotton dress that I should have changed when rosebuds bloomed after winter's icy end. But moths made Swiss cheese of it. Holes in hearts, holes in stomachs, & memories.

Is that the cat scratching under the door? Yes, but outside my dreams. Ignore the knocking. My conscience tells me they're uninvited guests. I feel the aching to remember that time we all fell into the bonfire. Thankfully, it had l o n g since burned out. We ran around with soot on our faces. Smeared & smiling we all were. Where are you now?

It is better to say *"Always Remember"* or *"Never Forget"*? One's a double negative, my friend. A Negative. Is forgetting a form of ignoring? I think ignoring is harder than ignorance to pull off. One more of anything is a nightmare missing its happy ending. The scrolling continues...The question in life is no longer *"What's the meaning?"* but *"What's that from?"*

Even in our sleep we can generate s t r e ss just by learning to snore. On the sheets: my deep reds & light browns—leaves from trees—all waiting still for Spring's rinse cycle to bloom again.

Strange. Waking in a pool of my own slobber, dreaming I d r o w n e d. Waking to wonder where you are. Surrounded by the obscurity of so much light. The sun rose this morning & it hurt my eyes even when I closed them. Still orange glows under my lids. The scrolling continues...

When You Read And Write Every Day And That Becomes A Nightcap, Which You're Grateful For Then You Read *Consider This* by Chuck Palahniuk And You Cry Because Everything Seems To Suddenly Make Sense. And Even If It Doesn't Really, For the First Time In A Long Time You're Okay With It So You Write A Poem About *Being* That Becomes A Play On Words. Or It's Just A Poem About Yourself Again And You're Just Not Used to Being *You* Quite Yet. But You're Still, Like, "Whatever" Because You're Better Off Now Than You Were A Year Ago. And You'll Be Even More Better Off In Another.

On being a road

Pros: You're used every day.
Cons: You're used *every* day.

My children think they time travel when they fall asleep on long road trips. They're *not* wrong. I watch tumbleweeds roll over the road, then into fences holding back swaying grass. A tornado spins. Snow comes at my windshield like I'm flying the Millennium Falcon: white-knuckled and laughing. *All* while they snore in the backseat.

On being a cactus

Pros: No one *touches* you.
Cons: *No one* touches you.

Action carries its own authority. When someone says *desert* I always muse over the first person who ate a cactus. Were they *that* lucky the first time or just strong enough to withstand the spines and glochids on their tongue? There is as much power in doing something *wrong* as there is in doing *everything* right.

On being a good song

Pros: You're played over & over.
Cons: You're played. Over & over.

When you least expect it, a song becomes a corkscrew in your spine. Sometimes, music leads me to lean on the wall in a dark room. Clenching fists until crescent moons line my palms like ocean tides. Other times, I hold visions of Jurassic era ammonites all the way through the extinction of the Northern White Rhinoceros in my ears. My temple throbs and I'm filled cheek-to-jowl with joy.

On being yarn

Pros: There's *no control* over what you're made into.
Cons: There's no control over what *you're* made into.

If I run out of yarn before finishing a scarf, my fingers—and for a moment, even my mind—sit quietly in an uncomfortable moment of *nothing*. Lingering in the space around silence as if it's a cup of coffee brewing. I often say to myself, "It must be seven minutes past the hour somewhere." Too bad I didn't know until *today* that it's *possible* Jesus Christ and Abraham Lincoln *both* died seven minutes past the hour. *Maybe* we fall—like a purl stitch—into silence, to acknowledge *those* moments.

On being a good book

Pros: Pages are dog-eared *forever*.
Cons: Pages are dog-eared. Forever.

Writers just need to list the rules and make sure they become *mutually* agreed upon. Kids can make *any* world real: the floor is lava and sticks conquer dragons. Afterall, it *was* a man-child who stuffed a clock into an alligator. It was *magic* that turned carriages back into pumpkins for that *already* poor teenage girl. Readers *love* that shit.

On being sunglasses

Pros: You dim the light!
Cons: You *dim the* light.

The opposite of seeing is *not* seeing. The opposite of caring is *not* caring. The opposite of *love* is not *hate*. It's apathy because hate contains as much passion as love. All I can think about are the synonyms for *loyal* and how the family dog ate the sunglasses my husband bought for me the day he admitted to having an affair. He stopped chewing the couch after my soon-to-be-ex-husband moved out. The opposite of listening is *not* talking. Maybe, when it gets hard, the synonym for listening is *waiting to talk*.

On being hair

Pros: You're mostly dead anyway, so *have fun!*
Cons: You're mostly *dead anyway*. So, have fun?

Montaigne once said something like, "Freedom and restriction are the same thing." So, I started dyeing my hair because I thought I *could* control that. Every time my strands come out green or orange, I learn to accept what I *can't* control. I learn that *freedom* lets me change back.

On being a solar flare

Pros: You *burst* in & out, still enjoying the unexplainable.
Cons: You burst in & *out*. Still taking joy. It's all unexplainable.

Every January, I sit down with a wall calendar and mark each predicted meteor shower for the year. But it always ends up cloudy on those starry nights, so I'll never *know* for sure. I don't see a way to untangle all our pasts—all those days we missed a solar flare with our bare eyes. I also realize poets write for other poets, so I'll leave that explanation for tomorrow.

When You Write a Poem Called "Just Enough" Then Turn It Into A Song Because You Were Told To "Just Try Making A Song" Even Though You Don't Play Any Instruments And Can't Carry A Tune To Save Your Life. But You Can Write In Rhyme Even Though You Hate To Write Poetry That Rhymes. Late One Night, You Clink A Spoon On A Coffee Cup Synced Over A Blues Beat And Now There's This Song That Exists And No One Will Ever Hear It. But You Get To Read My Pop Song Like It's A Hallmark Card.

In the simple search for relief,
some find love, some find grief.
Pass the test, play the game.
We're all happy & hurting just the same.

Sometimes we struggle to get it straight:
laughter & pain, love & hate.
We fight to stir things up.
We make believe—we make things up.

If you live & love
then you know, feelings tend to come & go.
Some are weak, some are tough.
Let's open up & see that's just enough.

Sometimes it helps to hang on
but it won't resolve the right or wrong.
Today we're here.
The next we could be gone.

Is life complete?
Maybe, but it's not too long.
Sometimes it helps to hang on
but won't resolve the right or wrong.

If you live & love
then you know, feelings always come & go.
Some are weak, you will be tough.
You will open up; you will see that's just enough.

If you live & love
you know, feelings tend to come & go.
Some are weak, I will be tough.
I'll open up & see how I'm just enough.

How we're all just enough.
If we live & love—
that's just enough.
Just enough.

When You Leave Fingerprint Ink Stains On A Sofa During An Open Mic And It's Okay Because That's A Time You Said, "Sorry" And Were Really Forgiven. Looking Back, You Think Maybe Everyone Was Too Drunk To Care Or They Were Too Busy Rewriting Their Own History And That Just Reminds You Of A Hemingway Quote: "Write Drunk, Edit Sober." There's No Relevance Except Poets Need To Always Watch What They Say Because Something You Stupidly Express Or Do When Drunk Could Become Your Legacy. At Least My Mistake Is Just A Fingerprint, Not A Quote. Or Maybe This Collection Is Just One Big *Oops* Or You're Used To Living In That Meta-Poetic Space Now.

A poet's fingerprints
are more than stains crinkling paper.
We speak for the trees:
Writing between their rings—
Endless expressions on a new page.

Swirling words to paint with onyx pigment
fill the space between thought & time
heartbeat & rhyme. The tools are ancient—
papyrus filled with hieroglyphics
tell the story of who we were
& what's to come in the afterlife.
Wrapped in eternity with hearts
in jars & scratches on a sarcophagus.

Time travels to ink quills
dipped & bleeding on scrolls
unraveling secrets & spells
or declarations & rejections.

A poet's fingerprints
are more than ink stains crinkling paper.
Flummoxed ancestors telling us to ignite the fire
with verbs & embers.
To write our wisdom before we forget.

Flames whisper up a poet's nose:
"Don't let the trees die in vain."
So, we fill empty spaces with stories
& spill our blood across ink blots.
We own the rings of life—each line
is smoke blinding our insides.

A poet's fingerprints
are more than ink stains crinkling paper.
We are the paper
sacrificed to the fire
for our word's survival.

When *Praise For Poets* Becomes An Obligation To Prove That Words Are As Important To Art As Paintings On Gallery Walls Because You Work With So Many Visual Artists Who Don't Understand What's It's Like To Create Images With Words, Symbols, And Synonyms Like Admire, Applaud, Approval, Celebrate, Compliment, Congratulate, Flatter, Revere.

Praise for the poets:
The ones with love like crimson—dried & peeling off their ribs—scraping away the bleeding. A need to be seen! *Soothing* the barren pages.

Praise for the pens:
The ones that show up without asking. *Oozing* what's on my mind—flowing through sunsets & abstractions. Challenging onyx: seeping ink right up to the edge of death—but ballpoints *always* come back for me! The pressure of a hard hand leaves traces—etchings on the paper beneath.

Praise for the hands:
The ones whose chorus sings between the lines. *Sinking* into creases—groaning for the truth of creation—heavy pleadings. Palms *clenched* then *open* to the sky reaching for the muses. Quietly mixing. Molding. Melding. Verbs & nouns: *love* & *loss* are actions. Verbs! Listen, now...*hear* the verbs.

Praise for the poets:
The ones who are punctuation on dark skies. Stars speckled across the pages. I don't always acknowledge myself as the medium—as the stardust but if I ever say it's not worth it—the night or the pen—I would be lying. I am more! *More* than my edits. *More* than pigment. I am self-evident. I am a poet!

When You're An Atheist But Write A Poem About Heaven Anyway Because One Of Your Favorite Poets, Sarah Manguso, Wrote One About Hell. You Remember Riding In An Elevator With Her Up To A Gallery In New York To Look At Photographs And She Said, "You're Not A Writer Unless You're Damaged." And You Never Wanted To Be Damaged But Somehow Nearly 20 Years Later You're Actually Thankful You're Able To Kintsugi Yourself Into The Poetry World. And Maybe That's What Heaven Is.

People roll their chins toward hell when praying into their hands but when cursing they raise their fists toward heaven.

Heaven is having a job and not having a job.

Heaven is a song no one knows how to play.

Heaven is not ripping off a Band-Aid, maybe it's the wound underneath.

Heaven is eating a chocolate bar when you're menstruating.

Heaven is making love, when you're in love.

Heaven is a morality costume some people wear.

Heaven is my eyes dilating in the sun.

Heaven is getting enough sleep, but is it a dream?

Heaven is a moment we're most ourselves.

I don't want to end with a cliché, but maybe that's what heaven is.

Acknowledgements

Versions of the following poems have appeared in these publications:

"Plums" (30)
Dreamstones of Summer: A summer poetry anthology by Wingless Dreamer
09/2021

"The Jackhammer of a Man" (58)
We Are The West: A Colorado Anthology
09/2022

"A Poet's Fingerprints" (98)
Dimepiece: Ten Years of CLI Poetry
05/2023

Portions of poems in this book have appeared on my Instagram: @word_nerd_ris

The sincerest thank you to Andrés Sánchez for being my mentor and guiding me through the inception of my poetry career.

About the Author

Marissa Forbes (she/her) is an artist, writer of all genres, a creative instructor, and mother. Her chapbook, *Surviving Peter Pan*, was published by Beyond the Veil Press. Forbes' full-length collection, *Bridging the Gap: Poems & Ethos for Emily Warren Roebling* is available through Finishing Line Press. Other published poems and short stories can be read on marissaforbes.com and @word_nerd_ris. She is the Managing Editor for *Twenty Bellows*, a Colorado based literary magazine, was awarded an Author Fellowship from Martha's Vineyard Institute of Creative Writing in 2021 and is a Pushcart Nominee for 2023. Forbes has resided all over the country but now lives a colorful life with her two children, Jack and Layne, her father, dog, and cat in Denver, Colorado.

Resources

DIAL 988 IN A CRISIS

WEBSITES

1. Active Minds—Mental health awareness and education for students: *activeminds.org*
2. Anxiety & Depression Society of America—Prevention, treatment, and cure of anxiety, depression, OCD, PTSD, and co-occurring disorders through education, practice, and research: *adaa.org*
3. The Trevor Project—Crisis intervention and suicide prevention services to lesbian, gay, bisexual, transgender, queer, and questioning youth: *thetrevorproject.org*
4. National Institute of Mental Health—Research on mental disorders: *nimh.nih.gov*

PODCASTS

1. *Where Is My Mind?* With Niall Breslin
2. *The Savvy Psychologist: Quick & Dirty Tips* with Dr. Monica Johnson
3. *The Hilarious World of Depression; Depreche Mode* with John Moe
4. *The Happiness Lab* with Dr. Laurie Santos
5. *Speaking of Psychology* with Kim I. Mills
6. *Being Well* with Dr. Rick Hanson and Forrest Hanson

APPS

Headspace: Meditation and Sleep Made Simple

www.ingramcontent.com/pod-product-compliance
Lightning Source LLC
Chambersburg PA
CBHW070149080526
44586CB00015B/1904